NODOSAURUS
and Other Dinosaurs of the East Coast

by Dougal Dixon

illustrated by
Steve Weston and **James Field**

PICTURE WINDOW BOOKS
Minneapolis, Minnesota

Picture Window Books
5115 Excelsior Boulevard
Suite 232
Minneapolis, MN 55416
877-845-8392
www.picturewindowbooks.com

Library of Congress Cataloging-in-Publication Data
Dixon, Dougal.
Nodosaurus and other dinosaurs of the East coast /
by Dougal Dixon ; illustrated by Steve Weston &
James Field.
p. cm. — (Dinosaur find)
Includes bibliographical references and index.
ISBN-13: 978-1-4048-2746-2 (hardcover)
ISBN-10: 1-4048-2746-3 (hardcover)
1. Nodosaurus—Juvenile literature. 2. Dinosaurs—
East (U.S.)—Juvenile literature. I. Weston, Steve, ill. II.
Field, James, 1959– ill. III. Title. IV. Series: Dixon, Dougal.
Dinosaur find.
QE862.O65D59 2007
567.90974—dc22   2006012135

Acknowledgments
This book was produced for Picture Window Books by
Bender Richardson White, U.K.

Illustrations by James Field (pages 4–5, 7, 9,
11, 19) and Steve Weston (cover and pages 13,
15, 17, 21). Diagrams by Stefan Chabluk.

Photographs: Eyewire Inc. pages 8, 12, 16; Digital
Vision page 18; iStockphoto pages 6, 14 (Janine
Bollinger), 20 (David Rose); Frank Lane Photo Agency
page 10 (Michael Quinton).

Consultant: John Stidworthy, Scientific Fellow of
the Zoological Society, London, and former
Lecturer in the Education Department, Natural
History Museum, London.

Reading Adviser: Susan Kesselring, M.A., Literacy
Educator, Rosemount–Apple Valley–Eagan
(Minnesota) School District

Types of dinosaurs

In this book, a red shape at the top of a left-hand page shows the animal was a meat-eater. A green shape shows it was a plant-eater.

Just how big—or small—were they?

Dinosaurs were many different sizes. We have compared their sizes to one of the following:

Chicken
2 feet (60 centimeters) tall
6 pounds (2.7 kilograms)

Adult person
6 feet (1.8 meters) tall
170 pounds (76.5 kg)

Elephant
10 feet (3 m) tall
12,000 pounds
(5,400 kg)

Table of Contents

What's Inside?

Dinosaurs! These dinosaurs lived on what is now the East Coast of North America. Find out how they survived millions of years ago and what they have in common with today's animals.

LIFE ON THE EAST COAST

Dinosaurs lived between 230 million and 65 million years ago. The world did not look the same then. At the beginning of this time, there was no Atlantic Ocean. North America was joined to Europe. What is now the East Coast was a desert area, right in the center of a continent.

Ammosaurus and herds of its relative, *Anchisaurus,* had to be careful at desert water holes. There were meat-eating *Podokesaurus* prowling around.

ANCHISAURUS

Pronunciation:
ANG-ki-SAW-rus

Anchisaurus was one of the first plant-eating dinosaurs. It roamed the desert plains in herds, looking out for meat-eaters that might attack it. It fed on the straggly plants that grew in the damper areas. It used its long neck to reach the plants.

Desert animals today

The jackrabbit lives in deserts, like *Anchisaurus* did. It, too, eats any straggly plants it comes across.

Size Comparison

6

Anchisaurus mostly moved on all four legs. It had big eyes and used its good sight to watch for predators like *Podokesaurus*.

AMMOSAURUS

Pronunciation:
AM-o-SAW-rus

Ammosaurus was a lot like *Anchisaurus.* It could walk on its hind legs or on all fours. It had big hands with strong digging claws. It used its claws to scrape in the desert sand for swollen roots and underground stems to eat.

Food digger today

The peccary lives on plant food buried in the ground. It uses its snout and hoofs to dig up food, like *Ammosaurus* did with its claws.

Size Comparison

8

Ammosaurus had to dig for its food. Lots of desert plants had deep roots and underground stems. They were protected from the heat of the sun and close to water beneath the sand.

PODOKESAURUS

Pronunciation:
POH-doh-kuh-SAW-rus

Podokesaurus was a small meat-eating dinosaur. It scampered over the deserts, leaving behind three-toed footprints. People have known of the fossil footprints for a long time and once thought they were the footprints of birds.

Fast feet today

When birds walk in mud, sand, or snow, they leave three-toed footprints just like those made by *Podokesaurus.*

10   Size Comparison

Podokesaurus hunted the small animals of the desert. If it had wanted to hunt the bigger dinosaurs, it would have done so in packs.

11

APPALACHIOSAURUS

Pronunciation: AP-al-LAY-chee-o-SAW-rus

At the end of the Age of Dinosaurs, the Atlantic Ocean had appeared. Eastern North America was hilly and forested. In the forests prowled big meat-eating dinosaurs like *Appalachiosaurus*—a cousin of huge, fierce *Tyrannosaurus*.

Fierce hunter today

The mountain lion stalks the North American forests hunting for prey, just like *Appalachiosaurus* once did.

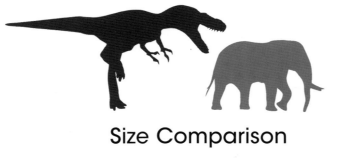

Size Comparison

12

Appalachiosaurus hid in the shadows of the forest, waiting for its prey to come along. Then—ambush!

Ornithomimus looked like a long-legged, long-necked bird. It used its long legs to run fast and its long neck to reach for food. It ate plant and animal food, including eggs, fruits, insects, and worms.

Long necks today

Whooping cranes are built like *Ornithomimus* was. They use their long necks to reach down and snatch prey.

Size Comparison

14

Ornithomimus lived along the East Coast between 76 million and 65 million years ago.

Hadrosaurus was one of the duck-billed dinosaurs. It had a broad, horny beak, or bill, as its mouth and jaws. It used this for tearing up big mouthfuls of plants, before chewing them with its strong, grinding back teeth.

Broad mouth today

Bison have broad mouths so that they can pull up and eat low-growing plants, like *Hadrosaurus* did.

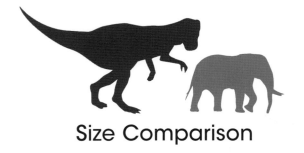

Size Comparison

16

Hadrosaurus was the first dinosaur to be discovered in North America. Sometimes, it would stand up on its hind legs to tear off plant food high above ground level.

LOPHORHOTHON

Pronunciation:
LOF-or-HOH-thon

Lophorhothon was a small duck-billed dinosaur. It had a short crest above the eyes, which it may have used to attract or signal other *Lophorhothon*. The color pattern on the dinosaur's sides helped it hide from meat-eaters.

Upright stance today

Lophorhothon was built like a prairie dog, and it probably stood upright in the same way to keep a lookout for predators.

Size Comparison

18

It was dangerous in the forests at the end of the Age of Dinosaurs. *Lophorhothon* had to watch out for the big meat-eaters like *Appalachiosaurus*.

NODOSAURUS

Pronunciation:
NOH-doe-SAW-rus

Nodosaurus was mostly covered in armor. It did not need to run fast to escape an attacker. It did not need to be camouflaged to hide from enemies. If attacked, *Nodosaurus* would have crouched close to the ground to protect its soft underbelly.

Armor today

A turtle is covered in armor. It is as well-protected from enemies as *Nodosaurus* was.

Size Comparison

20

Sometimes, even its tough armor couldn't protect *Nodosaurus* from fierce predators.

WHERE DID THEY GO?

Dinosaurs are extinct, which means that none of them are alive today. Scientists study rocks and fossils to find clues about what happened to dinosaurs.

People have different explanations about what happened. Some people think a huge asteroid hit Earth and caused all sorts of climate changes, which caused the dinosaurs to die. Others think volcanic eruptions caused the climate to change and that killed the dinosaurs. No one knows for sure what happened to all of the dinosaurs.

Glossary

armor—protective covering of plates, horns, spikes, or clubs used for fighting

bill—the hard front part of the mouth of birds and some dinosaurs; also called a beak

camouflage—patterns or colors on the skin that allow an animal to blend in with its surroundings so that it will not be noticed

continent—a huge area of land like North America and Asia

crest—a structure on top of the head, usually used to signal to other animals

desert—a usually hot, dry region with land covered in sand or stones

herds—large groups of animals that move, feed, and sleep together

packs—groups of animals that hunt and kill together

plains—large areas of flat land with few large plants

prey—animals that are hunted by other animals for food; the hunters are known as predators

23

To Learn More

At the Library

Clark, Neil, and William Lindsay. *1001 Facts About Dinosaurs.* New York: Backpack Books, Dorling Kindersley, 2002.

Dixon, Dougal. *Ornithomimus and Other Fast Dinosaurs.* Minneapolis: Picture Window Books, 2006.

Holtz, Thomas, and Michael Brett-Surman. *Dinosaur Field Guide.* New York: Random House, 2001.

On the Web

FactHound offers a safe, fun way to find Internet sites related to this book. All of the sites on FactHound have been researched by our staff.

1. Visit *www.facthound.com*
2. Type in this special code for age-appropriate sites: 1404827463

3. Click on the FETCH IT button.

Your trusty FactHound will fetch the best sites for you!

Index

Look for all of the books in the Dinosaur Find series: